Easy, Clean Meal Ideas For People on the Go!

Clean Plate, Fresh Slate

By

Christine C. Preston

CLEAN PLATE, FRESH SLATE

by
Christine C. Preston

Copyright 2020 ICHAMPION Publishing

Published by iCHAMPION Publishing
P.O. Box 2352 Frisco, TX 75034
Content edit by Nikia Hammonds-Blakely and iCHAMPION Publishing
Library of Congress Cataloging-in-Publication Data Publisher and Printing by iCHAMPION Publishing
Recipes Provided By: Christine C. Preston & iCHAMPION Publishing
Illustrated By: iCHAMPION Publishing
Cover Design By: Michele Pringle
ISBN: **978-1-7349212-8-1**
Categories: COOKBOOK
SELF HELP

This book is dedicated to my mother, Justine, who saw my name on a book cover before I believed it to be so.

A Million Thank You's to Angie & Isaac ("Three the Hard Way") for always encouraging me on this journey, as well as countless loved ones who reminded me, "You Can Do This!" To Nikia Hammonds-Blakely and iCHAMPION Publishing, I am eternally grateful for this opportunity, God's Richest & Continued Blessings to you!

Thank You

EGGPLANT PARMESAN

Ingredients:

- 2 Eggplants
- 2 Eggs
- 1/2 Diced Bell Pepper, 1/2 Diced Onion, & 1/2 Cup of chopped Mushrooms
- Almond Flour for dusting
- 1 Jar of Margherita Pizza sauce
- 1 Package fresh Mozzarella cheese cut into cubes
- 3/4 Cup grated Parmesean
- Small bunch of Dried Basil
- Seasoning Salt & Pepper, & Italian Seasoning for Seasoning

Method:

- Peel and thinly slice Eggplant (sprinkling a small amount of seasoning salt and pepper on each side), Set aside on towel to drain excess water, which helps with frying
- First, preheat oven to 350 degrees F.
- Saute' your bell peppers, onions, & mushrooms in olive oil, drain, & set to the side.
- Dip eggplant slices in egg, then lightly dust in almond flour & fry them in olive oil.
- Then spray baking dish w/Olive Oil Spray and spread Pizza Sauce all over it, evenly.
- Place eggplant slices in the sauce.
- Spread sautéed veggies over eggplant slices & sprinkle with Parmesan cheese.
- Top it with cubes of Mozzarella, basil and Parmesan cheeses.
- Repeat the layering process, For the top layer, spoon remaining sauce and cheese.
- Cover loosely with foil and bake for 20 min, remove foil and bake for another 20 min.
- Optional: Place under broiler for 3-5 min.

Don't be so hard on yourself!

VEGGIES WITH SMOKED TURKEY SAUSAGE

Ingredients:

- Smoked turkey sausage
- Tri-colored bell peppers
- Yellow onion
- Head of fresh broccoli or veggies of Your choice
- Olive oil
- Olive oil spray
- Pink himalayan sea salt
- Pepper

Method:

- Pre-heat Air Fryer to 370 degrees.
- Slice veggies, coat with olive oil and season.
- Spray air fryer with Olive oil cooking spray.
- Slice sausage and place in air fryer for 10-12 minutes.
- Then add veggies to sausage in air fryer for 10 minutes.
- And serve.

Never diminish your progress, no matter how small it appears.

FRIED CAULIFLOWER STEAKS

Ingredients:

- 1 Large cauliflower sliced into 1" thick steaks
- Olive oil for frying
- 1 Cup super fine almond flour
- 1 TSP Black pepper
- 1 TSP Garlic powder
- 1 TSP Onion powder
- 1 TSP Paprika
- 1 TSP Seasoning salt
- 3 Eggs

Method:

- Cut the cauliflower into slices about 1" in thick.
- In shallow bowl, whisk flour and seasonings.
- In another shallow bowl, beat eggs.
- Take a large frying pan and heat the oil on medium high heat.
- Toss cauliflower in flour mixture, then eggs, then in the flour mixture again.
- Carefully add cauliflower to oil and fry about 2 minutes on each side, until golden in color.
- Transfer it to serving plate and then serve with honey hot sauce (mix together 1 cup of honey and 2 tbs of hot sauce for a quick and easy sauce).

You got this, because God's got you!

FRIED ZUCCHINI STEAK FRIES

Ingredients:

- 4 Medium sized zucchini
- 3 Eggs
- Salt
- Black pepper
- 1 Cup Super fine almond flour
- Olive oil
- ¼ Cup parsley leaves, chopped

Method:

- Cut zucchini into fry like sticks.
- Take a bowl, add eggs w/salt and pepper, then beat ingredients together.
- Take a separate plate, & fill with almond flour.
- Take zucchini fries & coat with egg, then flour.
- Put olive oil in a large pan on medium heat. When oil is fully heated, carefully place zucchini pieces in oil and fry for 3 minutes (or until golden and crispy).
- Garnish with parsley, lightly sprinkle with salt, and Enjoy.

Faith Forward

OATMEAL SWEET POTATO BARS

Ingredients:

- 1 Cup mashed sweet potato (I used a left over baked sweet potato)
- 1 TSP Baking powder
- 1 TSP Cinnamon
- 2 Cups of rolled oats
- 1/2 TSP Sea salt
- 1/4 cup of honey
- 2 Cups of Unsweetened vanilla almond milk
- 1 TBS Vanilla Whey Protein Powder

Topping:

- 1/4 Cup Chopped pecans
- 2 TBS Of rolled oats
- 1 TBS Melted coconut oil
- 1/4 Cup erithrytol sugar substitute

Method:

- First preheat oven to 375 degrees F.
- Spray 8 inch square baking dish with olive oil cooking spray.
- In large bowl mix oats, baking powder, cinnamon, salt, stir.
- Add milk, sweet potato, honey, coconut oil, and vanilla protein powder & mix.
- Carefully pour mixture into baking dish
- Mix together topping ingredients and sprinkle over oatmeal mixture, sprinkle with cinnamon & spray with olive oil cooking spray.
- Bake for 30 - 35 minutes until top is golden and center is set.
- Optional, drizzle with honey after cutting.

Keep
Going, It's
So Worth It

SWEET POTATO CINNAMON STICKY MUFFINS

Ingredients:

- 1 Cup mashed sweet potato
- 1 Cup erithrytol sugar substitute - divided
- 1/4 Cup olive oil
- 1/2 Cup vanilla unsweetened almond milk
- 2 large eggs
- 1 TSP Vanilla
- 1 Cup super fine almond flour
- 1 Cup old-fashioned oats (not instant)
- 1 TSP cinnamon- divided
- 1/2 TSP pumpkin pie spice
- 2 TSP Vanilla whey protein powder
- Pinch of salt

Method:

- Preheat oven to 350 degrees.
- Prepare a 12 muffin pan with muffin paper cups, and lightly coat with cooking spray.
- Whisk together sweet potato, 1/2 cup Erithrytol , olive oil, milk, eggs, and vanilla in a large bowl. Add oats and almond flour. Whisk until smooth and well combined.
- Add and mix in 3/4 teaspoon of cinnamon, pumpkin pie spice, protein powder, and salt.
- Fill each muffin cup 1/2 way with the muffin mixture
- In a small bowl, combine the remaining 1/4 teaspoon of cinnamon, and remaining 1/2 cup of Erithrytol and pecans.
- Top each muffin with a generous sprinkle of the pecan mixture.
- Bake for 22 to 25 minutes, or until the toothpick comes out clean.
- Drizzle with honey.

You're So Much Stronger Than You Think

HONEY PECAN BAKED SWEET POTATO WITH VEGAN BUTTER AND CINNAMON

Ingredients:

- 2 Pounds sweet potatoes
- Vegan butter
- 3 TBSP Honey
- 1 1/2 TSP Cinnamon
- 1/4 Cup pecans
- 1-2 TBSP Brown sugar

Method:

- Preheat oven to 425F. On a baking sheet, (lined with foil for easy clean-up if you wish) prick sweet potatoes all over with a fork & coat with Olive Oil.
- Bake until tender, or until a fork inserted in the thickest part has no resistance, 45 to 50 minutes.
- Let cool, then split the tops open with a knife. Place vegan butter in the center, sprinkle with cinnamon, chopped pecans, & honey
- Optional: Place under broiler for 1-3 min

I Love You

CAST IRON SEARED COD WITH HONEY LIME SLAW

Ingredients:

FOR THE FISH:

- 1 1/2 LBS Cod
- 1 1/2 TSP Chili powder
- 1/2 TSP Cumin
- 1/2 TSP Garlic powder
- 1/2 TSP Onion powder
- 1/2 TSP Smoked paprika
- 1/2 TSP Salt
- 1 1/2 TBSP Avocado oil

FOR THE HONEY LIME SLAW:

- 1 Package of tri colored slaw mixture
- 1 TBS honey
- 2 limes (squeeze juice)
- 1/2 TSP sea salt and pepper

Method:

- Take a small bowl and mix cumin, onion powder, chili powder, garlic powder, salt and smoked paprika.
- Place fish in a container and coat with the seasoning.
- Take a pan and heat the oil. Then cook fillets for 4 minutes.
- For the making of honey lime slaw mix all the ingredients and then set aside.

For Assembly

Place fish, slaw, and black or brown rice in a bowl, garnish with fresh pico, lime, jalapenos, and enjoy

You're a
RockStar!

CAST IRON CAULIFLOWER PIZZA CRUST

Ingredients:

- 1 Medium to large head of cauliflower
- 2 Eggs
- 1 Cup grated/shredded mozzarella cheese or favorite pizza cheese blend
- 1/2 Cup of grated parmesan cheese from the can
- 1 TSP Garlic powder
- 1/2 TSP Dried oregano
- 1/2 TSP Dried basil
- Pinch of salt and pepper

Method:

- Preheat oven to 425° and line a sheet pan with parchment paper.
- Grate the head of cauliflower to a minced/riced consistency.
- Microwave cauliflower in a microwave-safe bowl for 5 minutes. This will tenderize the vegetable.
- Let cool until cool enough to handle. Place cauliflower in a kitchen towel and squeeze as much water out as possible.
- Place ball of squeezed cauliflower in a mixing bowl and add the cheeses, eggs, and spices. Mix until thoroughly combined.
- Spray your cast iron skillet generously with Olive Oil Cooking Spray
- Pour contents into the skillet. Press into a circle shape, making sure to make a little lip at the edge of the crust.
- Bake 20 minutes until crust is brown and more firm. (Additional baking time may be needed, until the crust is to your preferred firmness - if so, bake in additional increments of 5-7 minutes at a time).
- Top with favorite sauce and pizza toppings. Bake for another 10-15 min until cheese is melted and browned.
- Optional: Place under broiler for 5 minutes.

Don't Stop

SALMON SPINACH WRAP

Ingredients:

- 1 Skinless salmon filet
- 1 Gluten free spinach tortilla wrap
- 1/2 Cup sliced red bell pepper
- 1/2 Cup of Fresh Spinach
- 1/2 Cup diced red onion
- 1/2 Cup of shredded cheese of your choice
- Banana peppers

Method:

- Season your Salmon on both sides.
- Heat Olive Oil in Skillet and add sliced red bell peppers and sautee.
- Then add salmon to the pan, and sear for 4 minutes on both sides.
- In a separate pan, spray olive oil cooking spray, and heat; then place spinach wrap in pan, browning on both sides.

To assemble:

- Place shredded cheese on spinach wrap, then add salmon, red bell peppers, fresh spinach, and red onions, sprinkle w/sea salt and pepper, and add banana peppers.

Optional:

- Fold wrap, spray with olive oil cooking spray, and place in oven on 350 degrees for 5-7 minutes, to melt the cheese.

You're So Much Closer Than You Think

TURKEY BURGERS

Ingredients:

- 1 LB Ground turkey
- 1 Egg
- 2 TBS Minced Garlic
- 1 TBSP Worcestershire sauce
- 2 TBSP Parsley
- Seasoning salt
- Black pepper
- Onion powder
- Garlic powder
- Paprika
- 1/2 Diced yellow onion
- 1/2 Diced bell pepper
- Extra-virgin olive oil

Method:

- Sautee your onions and bell peppers in olive oil for 5 minutes.
- Take a large bowl & mix ground turkey, the onion & bell pepper mixture, your eggs, seasonings, garlic, & Worcestershire.
- Then form patties from your mixture.
- Take a cast iron skillet and coat with Olive Oil and heat on Medium-High Heat.
- Add patties and cook until they turn golden.
- Serve on lettuce and top with your favorite veggies and sauce.

You Were
Built For This

TURKEY KIELBASA AND SPINACH SCRAMBLE

Ingredients:

- 1 Turkey kielbasa link
- Sliced tri-colored bell peppers
- 2 Eggs
- 1 Cup of Fresh spinach
- Seasoning salt
- Black pepper
- Crushed red pepper flakes
- Olive oil cooking spray

Method:

- Slice your turkey sausage. In a pan, sauté your bell peppers and sausage (You want to sauté the sausage until it is browned).
- Remove this mixture from the pan and add your spinach, season, then sauté until wilted.
- Remove this mixture from the pan and scramble your eggs (seasoned with seasoning salt and black pepper).

To Plate:

Place the scrambled eggs on on your dish, and top with the sautéed spinach, next to the eggs, place the sausage and pepper mixture, sprinkle the spinach and eggs with crushed red pepper flakes, and garnish with fresh pico de gallo.

The world became
a better place
the day
you were born

AIR FRYER CHICKEN FAJITA SALAD

Ingredients:

- ◆ 2 Boneless chicken breasts sliced
- ◆ 2-3 TBS of Fajita seasoning (1 TBS chilli powder, 2 tsp ground cumin, 2 tsp paprika, 2 tsp garlic powder, 2 tsp onion powder, 1 tsp black pepper, 1 tsp seasoning salt, 1/4 tsp of cayenne "optional")
- ◆ 1 Green bell pepper sliced
- ◆ 1 Red bell pepper sliced
- ◆ 1 Yellow bell pepper sliced
- ◆ 1 Small yellow onion sliced
- ◆ 2 Cups of Spinach or
- ◆ Romaine Lettuce (or Both)

Method:

- ◆ Combine the sliced chicken, bell peppers, and onion in a bowl.
- ◆ Coat the mixture with olive oil and add the fajita seasoning mixture - toss to combine.
- ◆ Heat your air fryer to 360 degrees.
- ◆ Spray your air fryer basket with olive oil cooking spray.
- ◆ Add the chicken and veggie mixture to the air fryer tray for 16-20 minutes, opening the air fryer and tossing the mixture once at the 10 minute mark.
- ◆ Once the fajitas finish cooking, serve over Chopped Swiss chard (or spinach or romaine lettuce) and garnish with avocado, tomatoes, shredded cheese, and fresh lime. Drizzle your salad with a pre-made cilantro lime vinaigrette dressing.

You deserve
to see your
dreams come true!

HONEY BALSAMIC SWEET POTATOES & VEGGIES

Ingredients:

- 2 Medium-sized sweet potatoes
- 1 Red bell pepper
- 1 Red onion
- 1 Yellow squash
- 1 Zucchini
- 1 Head of broccoli
- Extra virgin olive oil
- Garlic herb sea salt
- Ground pepper
- Garlic powder
- Onion powder
- Balsamic vinegar
- Honey

Method:

- Preheat oven to 425 F.
- Line baking sheet with parchment paper and spray with olive oil cooking spray.
- Cut up the sweet potatoes, coat with olive oil and drizzle honey and cinnamon on them. Place sweet potatoes on baking sheet and roast for 15 minutes.
- Coat and season the remaining veggies.
- Add remaining veggies to the sweet potatoes on the baking sheet and mix.
- Drizzle entire mixture with Balsamic Vinegar.
- Roast for an additional 20 minutes or until all veggies are at your preferred consistency.

You deserve every great thing coming your way!

AIR FRYER HONEY LEMON
PEPPER CHICKEN STRIPS

Ingredients:

- 8 Chicken tenderloins
- 2 Cups of super fine almond flour
- 2 Eggs
- Olive oil spray
- Garlic pepper sea salt
- Black pepper
- Garlic powder
- Onion powder
- Lemon pepper
- Honey

Method:

- Preheat Air Fryer to 370 degrees.
- Combine Seasonings (except Lemon Pepper) and toss chicken strips in the seasoning mixture.
- In one bowl, place the Almond Flour. In another bowl, beat the eggs.
- Dredge the chicken in the egg, then your almond flour - COMPLETELY coating the chicken.
- Spray your air fryer basket with olive oil cooking spray.
- Place 4 chicken strips in the basket and spray with olive oil cooking spray.
- Air Fry for 14 -20 minutes total - flipping and re-coating your strips with olive oil spray at the 7min mark.
- Air fry until strips are golden brown.
- Repeat above steps for your second batch of strips.
- Once strips are done, lightly sprinkle with lemon pepper seasoning and drizzle with honey.
- Serve with a Salad or Vegetable of your choice.

I am so proud of you!

AIR FRYER BUFFALO
CHICKEN STRIPS

Ingredients:

- 1 LB Chicken breasts cut into strips
- 1 Egg beaten
- 1/2 Cup super fine almond flour
- 1 TSP Seasoning salt
- 1 TSP Black pepper
- 1 TSP Garlic powder
- 1 TSP Onion powder
- 1/2 Cup Hot sauce
- 1/2 TBS Vegan butter
- Olive oil cooking spray

Method:

- Pre-heat Air Fryer to 370 degrees.
- Place beaten egg in shallow bowl.
- Mix Almond Flour and Seasonings in a shallow bowl.
- Spray the air fryer basket with olive oil cooking spray.
- Cut chicken breasts into strips.
- Place chicken into egg mixture, then coat with flour mixture.
- Place strips in air fryer and coat with olive oil cooking spray.
- Fry for 8 minutes, flip, coat with spray and fry for an additional 8 minutes.
- While the chicken is in the air fryer, warm your hot sauce and vegan butter in a small sauce pan.
- Remove chicken from air fryer and carefully toss in buffalo sauce.
- Serve alongside the veggies of your choice and enjoy.

Never diminish
your progress,
no matter how
small it appears.

CHICKEN AND VEGGIE FOIL MEAL

Ingredients:

- Olive oil
- Seasoning salt, black pepper, onion powder, garlic powder, paprika, Italian seasoning
- 1 Large chicken breast
- 1/2 Sliced yellow bell pepper
- 1/2 Sliced yellow onion
- 1 Zucchini
- 3 Small yellow potatoes (optional)
  *Feel free to add any of your favorite veggies

Method:

- Preheat your oven to 425 degrees.
- Spread out a piece of foil on a sheet pan
- Spray the foil generously with Olive Oil cooking spray.
- Clean and slice your chicken breast.
- Clean and cut your veggies.
- Place chicken and veggies in a bowl, coat in olive oil, season, and toss so that oil and seasonings are on full mixture.
- Spread chicken and veggies on foil and fold closed, tightly.
- Bake for 40-50 minutes.
- Carefully open foil and broil for 2-3 minutes, then serve.
  *This serving is for one person, for multiple servings, make several foil packets
- Enjoy.

You got this, because God's got you!

BAKED CHICKEN WINGS

Ingredients:

- ♦ 1 LB of Chicken Wings or Wingettes
- ♦ Olive oil
- ♦ Olive oil cooking spray
- ♦ Black pepper pink sea salt (or seasoning salt of your choice)
- ♦ Black pepper
- ♦ Garlic powder
- ♦ Onion powder
- ♦ Paprika
- ♦ Wing sauce of your choice

Method:

- ♦ Preheat your oven to 400 Degrees.
- ♦ On a baking sheet, spread out a piece of parchment paper or aluminium foil (for easy clean up). Spray the parchment paper/foil with olive oil cooking spray.
- ♦ Clean your wings and dry throughly by lining them on a kitchen safe towel and patting dry.
- ♦ Get a large bowl, place all wings in the bowl, coat with olive oil, and season.
- ♦ Thoroughly toss the wings in the olive oil and seasonings so that each wing is coated.
- ♦ Line your wings on the prepared baking sheet
- ♦ Bake on 400 degrees for 40-50 minutes (depending on the way you like your wings cooked). Turn your wings and spray with olive oil spray at the half way point.
- ♦ After wings are finished baking, place wings in a bowl, toss them in your favorite sauce.
- ♦ Line wings back on your prepared baking sheet and bake for 10 additional minutes. Enjoy.

Better is
coming!

ONE SKILLET CAJUN CHICKEN, SHRIMP, CHICKEN ANDOUILLE SAUSAGE, AND VEGGIES

··· ――――――――――――――――――――――――――― ···

Ingredients:

- 8 OZ Shrimp peeled, deveined, and tails removed
- 8 OZ Chicken andouille sausage (may also use chicken or turkey smoked sausage)
- 2 TBS Olive oil
- 1 Small Yellow onion, chopped
- 1 Red bell pepper, chopped
- 1 Green bell pepper chopped
- 1 Head of broccoli, chopped
- 1 Zucchini, chopped
- 1 TBS Minced garlic
- 1/4 Cup of chicken or vegetable broth
- 2 TSP of Cajun Seasoning (Pre made; or 2 tsp of each - paprika, garlic powder, oregano, seasoning salt, onion powder, ground pepper, cayenne)

Method:

- In a saute pan over medium heat, add 1 TBS of olive oil and your minced garlic - saute for 3 minutes.
- Season your prepared shrimp with the cajun seasoning and cook in olive oil and garlic for 2-3 minutes, flip and cook for one more minute.
- Once shrimp turns opaque and curl up, transfer to a plate, cover with foil, and set aside. Add remaining olive oil to pan, add veggies, EXCEPT ZUCCHINI, and sausage to pan and cook for 3-4 minutes (until sausage is brown and onions are translucent).
- Add Zucchini and broth to pan, scraping the bottom of the pan to deglaze.
- Cover the pan and reduce the heat to low and simmer for 3 minutes.
- Remove the lid, add Shrimp, and stir.

Keep Going, It's So Worth It

GARLIC GREEN BEANS WITH
MUSHROOMS AND CHERRY TOMATOES

Ingredients:

- 1 Package of fresh green beans
- 1 Package of sliced mushrooms
- 1 Package of cherry tomatoes, sliced
- 2 TBS of Minced garlic
- 1 Shallot
- Black pepper
- Sea salt
- Italian seasoning
- Olive oil

Method:

- Wash and Dry your Veggies (Keep all veggies separate).
- Toss green beans in olive oil and seasoning in a bowl, set aside.
- Take 1 TBS of olive oil and heat in a pan over medium/high heat.
- Add your Minced Garlic and shallot to the pan and saute for 2 minutes.
- Then, add your mushrooms to the garlic and shallot and sauté for 5 minutes (or until tender).
- Remove your mushroom and shallot mixture from the pan, set aside and cover.
- Add your seasoned green beans to the pan and saute for 5 minutes (or until they are at your desired consistency).
- Add your mushrooms and onions back to the pan, as well as your cherry tomatoes.
- Add 1 TBS of vegetable broth, cover, and let simmer on low for 5 minutes.
- Enjoy.

You're So
Much Stronger
Than You Think

COLLARD GREEN SALAD

... ——————————————————————————————— ...

Ingredients:

- 1-2 bunches of Collard Greens, Cleaned and trimmed
- 1 Red Onion, Cut
- 1 Yellow Bell Pepper, Cut
- 1 Red Bell Pepper, Cut
- 1 Red Onion, Cut
- 1/2 Cup of Walnuts (Optional)
- 1/2 Cup of Feta Cheese (Optional)
- Sea Salt
- Black Pepper
- Minced Garlic
- 1/2 Cup of Olive Oil
- 3 TBS Apple Cider Vinegar
- 2 TBS Dijon Mustard
- 4 TBS Honey

Method:

- Throughly Wash Your Greens, Chop, and Drain
- Blanch your greens (bring salted water to a rolling boil, add greens for 3-5 minutes (or to your desired tenderness), remove and add to cold water, drain and set aside)
- Dressing Mixture: In a bowl, Mix Olive Oil, Minced Garlic, Apple Cider Vinegar, Dijon Mustard, and Honey - Set Aside
- In a large bowl, add blanched greens and bell peppers, and Dressing Mixture - Toss so that all veggies are coated evenly with dressing, season with black pepper and sea salt as you prefer
- Top Salad with Red Onion, Feta Cheese, Walnuts.
- Enjoy

You're a
RockStar!

SHEPHERD'S PIE WITH MASHED CAULIFLOWER

Ingredients:

- 1 LB Of Ground Turkey
- 2-3 Packages of Frozen mashed cauliflower
- 1 Yellow Onion
- 1 Stalk of Celery
- 3 Green Onions
- 1 Package of Frozen Diced Peas and Carrots
- Garlic Pepper Pink Himalayan Seasoning Salt
- Onion Powder
- Garlic Powder
- Paprika
- Black Pepper
- Olive Oil
- Olive oil Cooking Spray
- Casserole Dish

Method:

- Preheat your oven to 400 Degrees.
- Spray a casserole dish with Olive Oil Spray and set aside.
- Bake the frozen mashed cauliflower for 20 minutes while you complete the following steps.
- Add 2 TBS of Olive Oil to a pan on Medium/Hight Heat.
- Once your oil is hot, add your yellow onion, garlic, celery, and Ground Turkey. Season your Onion, Garlic, and Ground Turkey mix with the seasonings listed.
- Once your meat is brown and the onions are translucent, transfer this mixture to your greased casserole dish, spreading evenly as the bottom layer.
- Take your frozen peas and carrots and add to your pan where you browned your ground turkey, and sauté for 5 minutes, to take the chill off of the veggies.
- Take these peas and carrots and spread evenly over the Ground Turkey mixture.
- Take your Mashed Cauliflower out of the oven, combining all packages in a bowl, and mix until smooth.
- Take the mashed cauliflower and spread it evenly over your meat and veggie layers.
- Sprinkle the top of the cauliflower with black pepper and spray the top of the cauliflower with olive oil.
- Bake for 35-40 minutes (or until your mashed cauliflower has started to brown around the edge of your casserole dish).
- Optional Step: Sprinkle the Shepherd's Pie with shredded cheese and place under the broiler for 5 min, or until the cheese is melted and golden brown.
- Garnish with sliced Green Onions.
- Enjoy.

I Love You

BAKED VEGGIE OMELETTE

Ingredients:

- 8 Eggs
- 1/2 Cup of Milk
- 1 Cup of shredded Cheddar Cheese (optional)
- 1/2 Cup of diced onion
- 3/4 Cup of red and green diced bell pepper
- 1/2 Cup of fresh spinach, chopped
- 1/2 Cup of diced mushrooms
- Seasoning salt and black pepper (to your preference)

Method:

- Preheat the oven to 400 Degrees.
- Spray a 9x9 inch baking dish with Olive Oil cooking spray.
- Whisk eggs and milk together in a large bowl.
- Add veggies and cheese to the egg mixture.
- Season the mixture with seasoning salt and black pepper and mix.
- Pour the egg mixture into your prepared baking dish.
- Bake for 35 minutes, or until the top turns light brown.
- Optional Step: Add more shredded cheese to the top and place under the broiler for 5 minutes. To Serve: Spread the Salsa of your choice on a plate, then cut a piece of the omelette and enjoy.

You're So Much Closer Than You Think

SIMPLE AIR FRYER SALMON

Ingredients:
- 1 Salmon Filet
- Olive Oil
- Olive Oil Cooking Spray
- Black Pepper Pink Himalayan Sea Salt
- Black Pepper
- Garlic Powder
- Onion Powder
- Old Bay Seasoning

Method:
- Preheat Air Fryer to 400 Degrees.
- Wash and Dry your Salmon Filet.
- Coat With Olive Oil.
- Season with Seasonings listed (feel free to add and/or omit).
- Spray your air fryer basket with olive oil cooking spray.
- Place salmon filet in basket and cook for 6 minutes.
- Open air fryer, flip filet and coat with more olive oil spray
- Fry for an additional 6-7 minutes.
- Enjoy.

You Can!

SWEET AND SAVORY
STUFFED ACORN SQUASH

Ingredients:

- 2 Acorn Squash, cut in half
- Vegan Butter
- 1 Cup of Black Rice, Cooked
- 1 Cup of Mushrooms, Diced
- 1 Cup of Red Bell Peppers, Diced
- 1/2 cup of Celery, Diced
- 1/2 Onion, Diced
- 1 TBS Minced Garlic
- Salt and Black Pepper to taste
- 1 TBS Olive Oil
- Olive Oil Spray

Method:

- Preheat your oven to 400 Degrees .
- Wash and dry your veggies .
- Cut your Acorn Squash in Half.
- Spread Parchment paper on a sheet pan and spray with olive oil cooking spray.
- Place 4 halves of Acorn Squash on the prepared sheet pan.
- Sprinkle the squash with salt and black pepper and place a tsp of vegan butter in the middle of each half.
- Spray each half with Olive oil cooking spray and roast in the oven for 50 minutes, or until fork tender.
- Cook one cup of black rice, as instructed on the package (use Chicken or Veggie Broth as your liquid).
- In a pan, heat 1 TBS of olive oil and 1 TBS of minced garlic on medium/high heat. Add your veggies to the pan and sauté until tender, and the onions are translucent.
- Add your cooked rice to the pan and season the mixture with Salt and Black Pepper to taste.
- Once squash is done, remove from oven and scoop 2 TBS of the rice and veggie mixture into the middle of the squash.

Made in the USA
Middletown, DE
05 January 2021